Original title:
Dreamcatcher's Journey

Copyright © 2024 Creative Arts Management OÜ
All rights reserved.

Author: Gideon Barrett
ISBN HARDBACK: 978-9916-90-604-0
ISBN PAPERBACK: 978-9916-90-605-7

Celestial Threads of Memory

In twilight's glow, the stars align,
We weave our dreams, a tale divine.
With whispers soft, the past unfolds,
In cosmic dance, our story holds.

Each glimmer shines, a breath of fate,
Time's gentle touch, we contemplate.
In silver threads, the heart does bind,
Through deep abyss, our hopes entwined.

The Flight of Enchanted Spirits

From ancient woods, they rise on high,
With wings of light, they touch the sky.
A melody of dreams takes flight,
Awakening the stars at night.

In whispered winds, their laughter swirls,
A dance of magic, our hearts unfurl.
With every beat, the world ignites,
In wondrous realms, where joy incites.

Patterns in the Night Sky

Constellations weave tales of old,
Each twinkling star, a wish retold.
In cosmic schematics, secrets lie,
As time drifts on, we gaze and sigh.

A tapestry of dreams we see,
In midnight's cloak, we find the key.
From past to present, futures blend,
In starlit whispers, we transcend.

Mirage of Lost Horizons

Beyond the dunes, in golden haze,
A phantom calls from distant bays.
With every step, the shadows tease,
Revealing paths beneath the trees.

In search of dreams, we wander far,
Chasing glimmers, like a star.
A fleeting glimpse of what could be,
In mirage's grip, we crave to see.

The Ritual of Twilight Flights

Across the skies where shadows play,
The whispers of the night hold sway.
With wings of dusk, we take our flight,
In the embrace of fading light.

A dance of stars, the moon's soft glow,
Guides the hearts where dreams do flow.
We rise with winds, through twilight's breath,
Embracing life, entwined with death.

Orbs of fire in velvety dark,
Trace the echoes of a lonesome lark.
In silence deep, our spirits wane,
Yet from the dusk, we rise again.

In every heartbeat, a pulse of time,
The ritual calls in nature's rhyme.
As night unveils its mystic sights,
We soar anew on twilight flights.

The Garden of Ethereal Dreams

In a garden where the shadows dance,
Whispers of fate weave a soft romance.
Petals flutter on the gentle breeze,
Carrying secrets among the trees.

Starlit blooms in colors bright,
Glow softly under the silver light.
Each fragrance tells a story old,
Of love that blossomed, tales retold.

The moonbeams weave through branches fine,
A tapestry of dreams divine.
In every leaf, a promise glows,
Of worlds uncharted where magic flows.

Time stands still in this sacred space,
In the embrace of nature's grace.
As echoes linger, let hearts ignite,
In the garden where dreams take flight.

The Heartbeat of Dreaming

In the stillness of night,
Whispers float like soft dew,
Each heartbeat a secret,
A world hidden from view.

Stars wink from above,
Guiding the paths we roam,
In the cradle of slumber,
We find our way back home.

Visions of colors dance,
Shadows cloak the bright light,
Dreams knit together threads,
Of hope, love, and delight.

Awake to the dawn's glow,
With echoes lingering near,
In the heartbeat of dreaming,
We hold what we hold dear.

Gossamer Threads of the Infinite

In the fabric of the sky,
Threads of silver weave tight,
Gossamer whispers woven,
In the tapestry of night.

Each star a point of fire,
In the vastness, we drift,
Bound by invisible lines,
In this celestial gift.

Dreams stretch beyond the veil,
Infinite paths unfold,
Connecting each soul's journey,
In stories yet untold.

Together we dance lightly,
On this fragile, bright seam,
With hearts wide open, we fly,
On gossamer threads of dream.

Spirits Dancing in Quietude

In the calm of the evening,
Soft shadows gently sway,
Spirits whisper in silence,
As the night guides their play.

Moonlight bathes the earth,
In silver, cool and bright,
All fears dissolve gently,
In the warmth of the night.

They twirl in the stillness,
With grace that's ever near,
Each movement tells a story,
As they dance without fear.

In quietude, they linger,
Embracing the vast sea,
Of memories and fragments,
In the spirit's jubilee.

Luminous Threads of Memory

In the weave of our past,
Luminous threads abound,
Each moment a sparkle,
In the fabric profound.

Faded photographs glimmer,
With stories left untold,
Captured in the silence,
As the years unfold.

Echoes of laughter linger,
In corners of the mind,
Each thread, a connection,
To the life we unwind.

With every tender heartbeat,
The memories draw near,
In luminous threads of love,
We hold what we hold dear.

Melodies of Enchanted Slumber

Whispers soft as twilight's kiss,
In the night, where dreams dare twist.
Echoes dance in shadows' grace,
Lulling hearts to a serene place.

Moonlight strokes the sleeping land,
Crafted by an unseen hand.
Stars align in peaceful array,
Guiding souls on their gentle way.

Each note hums a soothing tune,
Cradled by the silver moon.
Restful waters, calm and deep,
In enchanted slumber, we leap.

Hold the magic close and tight,
As we drift into the night.
With melodies so sweetly spun,
Our journey to the dawn begun.

In the Presence of Dreaming Light

A soft glow fills the dusky air,
Where hopes and visions freely share.
In the presence of a gentle flare,
Dreams take wing, light as a prayer.

Colors blend in twilight's seam,
Reality fades into a dream.
Cascading beams of whispered lore,
Invite the heart to seek and explore.

In this moment, time suspends,
On the path where magic bends.
Silence hums a sacred song,
In the light, we find where we belong.

Awake or sleeping, both are true,
In these realms, there's much to view.
In the presence of dreaming light,
We wander free, both day and night.

The Voyage of Untamed Thoughts

Waves of wonder, restless seas,
Carrying whispers on the breeze.
Thoughts embark on journeys unknown,
In the vastness, wild seeds are sown.

Navigating through twilight skies,
Ideas spark like fireflies.
With every twist, a tale unfolds,
In the night, adventure beholds.

Visions clash like storms at sea,
Untamed spirits long to be free.
In the swell, we lose our way,
Yet find our truth in disarray.

So set your sails to the uncharted,
Where fear and joy are intertwined.
The voyage sings, with heart ignited,
Untamed thoughts forever guiding.

Threads Woven in Silent Reverie

In the quiet of the night,
Dreams are spun, delicate and light.
Threads of silver woven tight,
In silent reverie, take flight.

Captured whispers float on air,
Secrets held with tender care.
Each loop holds a forgotten tale,
Carried softly like a sail.

Loops of memory intertwine,
Crafting moments so divine.
As dawn breaks with a gentle sigh,
Weaves of dreams lift gently high.

In this tapestry, we stand,
Language born from heart's own hand.
In silent reverie, we find,
All the beauty left behind.

Sails of Silk and Stardust

Upon the sea of twilight dreams,
We drift on sails of silk and beams.
Each star a whisper, soft and bright,
Guiding our hearts through the night.

With every wave, a story flows,
Of whispered hopes and secret throes.
The moon our compass, calm and wide,
We chase the tides with hearts as guide.

In fields where stardust gently falls,
We hear the echo of nature's calls.
The winds of fortune softly play,
As we navigate this cosmic sway.

To dance on whispers, soft and sleek,
In realms where light and shadows speak.
With every stroke upon the sail,
We journey forth, we shall not fail.

Through the Veil of Sleep

Through the veil of sleep we drift,
In dreams where shadows softly lift.
A tapestry of night unfolds,
In whispers of the starlit holds.

Each moment glows with hidden light,
Where fantasies take graceful flight.
A realm where time begins to bend,
And waking hours softly blend.

Drifting through the silken haze,
In rapturous nights that softly graze.
The essence of the twilight's breath,
In slumber's arms we flirt with death.

Awake to find the silence sweet,
In echoes of a heart's retreat.
Through the veil of life we roam,
In dreams we find our timeless home.

The Keeper of Nocturnal Secrets

In the hush of night, we meet,
The keeper waits with quiet feet.
With eyes that glimmer, wise and deep,
Guarding the secrets lovers keep.

Through the moonlight's gentle waltz,
Whispers of worlds where time halts.
Stories woven from soft sighs,
In shadows where the mystic lies.

Underneath the canopy's glow,
He guides the way where shadows flow.
A tapestry of tales untold,
In his embrace, the night unfolds.

With a smile that hides the key,
To all the dreams that long to be.
In sacred trust, he holds the night,
Where darkness dances with the light.

Journey Through the Enchanted Mist

In the embrace of gentle mist,
We wander where the shadows twist.
Every footfall soft as breath,
A pathway woven with hidden depth.

Through emerald glades and silver streams,
Lost in the fabric of our dreams.
The air, a melody so sweet,
As echoes guide our wandering feet.

In whispers soft, the forest stirs,
With ancient magic in its purrs.
Each glance reveals a tale anew,
In lands where wishes come to view.

Together we traverse the night,
With hearts alight, our souls take flight.
Through the mist we bravely roam,
In the enchanted land we find our home.

Dance of the Fleeting Mirages

In the desert's shimmering glare,
Figures waltz with a silent prayer.
Whispers of sand on a warm breeze,
Ghostly forms that tease and please.

Under the moon's watchful eye,
Mirages fade, then softly lie.
Hearts chase shadows, lost in flight,
Dancing dreams in the fading light.

With every step, a story spun,
Of distant lands and setting sun.
Footprints linger, then wash away,
In the sand where memories play.

Fleeting moments, time slips by,
As the stars begin to sigh.
A dance of hope, so swift and bright,
In the desert's endless night.

Cradled in Celestial Nets

Stars weave dreams in the dark,
Fires of the night leave their spark.
Galaxies swirl in a gentle embrace,
Cradling wishes in the vast space.

Comets race with a bright tail,
Through cosmic realms, they set sail.
Nebulae glow in colors divine,
Ethereal threads that intertwine.

Planets hum in a rhythmic tune,
Ballets play 'neath the watchful moon.
Childhood dreams float high above,
In nets of starlight, spun with love.

Boundless skies where hopes take flight,
Cradled softly in silver light.
Cosmic wonders in each breath,
Eternal dance, defying death.

Flickers of Hope in Twilight

As the sun dips low in the west,
Promises linger, a whispered jest.
Shadows stretch with a graceful sigh,
Painting dreams in the twilight sky.

Fireflies blink, a dance of delight,
Tiny sparks in the gathering night.
Each flicker tells of a wish reborn,
In the stillness, where hopes are torn.

With the dusk comes a tender sound,
Nature hushes, all around.
A serenade of what's yet to be,
In the silence, our hearts are free.

Though darkness envelops the fading day,
A gentle light will find its way.
For in the twilight, dreams softly gleam,
Flickers of hope in the midst of a dream.

The Lullaby of Soaring Dreams

In the cradle of night, thoughts take flight,
Wings of starlight, hearts feel light.
Whispers of wishes, soft as a sigh,
Lullabies sung to the moonlit sky.

Clouds drift gently, like boats on a stream,
Carrying secrets, crafting a dream.
Each note a promise, sweet and serene,
In the embrace of a night unseen.

With every heartbeat, we rise and we fall,
Echoes of dreams, the night's gentle call.
Soaring through realms where visions unite,
Beneath the blanket of shimmering light.

In this moment, all fear fades away,
As the stars guide us, night turns to day.
The lullaby of dreams softly hums,
As we embrace what tomorrow becomes.

Liquid Light

In shadows dance the flickering beams,
They weave a tale of silken dreams.
Each droplet glimmers, soft and bright,
A canvas painted with liquid light.

Through whispered winds, the echoes flow,
Where colors blend, and wonders grow.
In every heartbeat, a story ignites,
In the realm where we chase liquid light.

Waking Visions

In the dawn, when dreams take flight,
Awakening whispers banish the night.
Eyes blink open to the sun's embrace,
In waking visions, we find our place.

A tapestry woven with threads unseen,
Each moment a memory, serene and keen.
Guided by hope, we rise anew,
In the dance of life, where dreams come true.

Guardians of the Twilight Realm

Beneath the veil of the setting sun,
Guardians gather, the day is done.
In twilight's glow, they stand so tall,
Protecting secrets that enchant us all.

With silver wings and voices low,
They share the magic that we need to know.
In shadows deep, their wisdom shines,
Guardians whisper where the starlight binds.

Threads of Fate in the Dream World

In the dream world where shadows play,
Threads of fate twist night and day.
Every choice, a path anew,
In this realm, let dreams come true.

We stitch together our hopes and fears,
With laughter mixed in with the tears.
Beyond the veil of reality's hold,
The dream world's secrets silently unfold.

Celestial Whispers and Stardust Paths

Stardust paths in the velvet sky,
Celestial whispers as time floats by.
Among the stars, our spirits soar,
In cosmic dance, we seek for more.

Guided by light from worlds unknown,
In the symphony of night, we find our home.
With open hearts, we embrace the vast,
In celestial realms, forever cast.

In Search of the Hidden Realms

Beyond the veil where shadows play,
Ancient secrets hide away.
A flicker of light, a breath of air,
Guides the heart to wander there.

In the woods where silence sings,
Mysteries dance on whispered wings.
Beneath the stars, a path unfolds,
To hidden realms and tales untold.

Through misty dreams, we lose our sense,
Reality bends, a shifting fence.
Here in the dark, new worlds ignite,
In search of realms beyond our sight.

Each step we take, a story we weave,
In trails of magic, we dare believe.
The hidden realms await our call,
In twilight's hush, we brave them all.

Threads of Stardust and Twilight

In the tapestry of night, stars gleam,
Threads of stardust weave a dream.
With twilight's kiss, the world transforms,
As shadows dance in whispered forms.

Moonlit pathways stretch and sway,
Guiding wanderers on their way.
In every twinkle, secrets flow,
Across the skies, a gentle glow.

Beneath the cosmos, hearts align,
In unity, we seek the sign.
For in the darkness, hope takes flight,
We gather dreams on threads of light.

With every heartbeat, we connect,
Embrace the magic we expect.
In this vast universe, we'll find,
Threads of stardust intertwined.

Whispers of the Midnight Web

In shadows deep where silence breathes,
The midnight web weaves dreams like leaves.
A fragile thread, so finely spun,
Captures echoes of the night begun.

Beneath the moon's soft silver glow,
Whispers linger, moving slow.
Secrets shared in silent sighs,
Entwined in magic, 'neath starlit skies.

Each flickering light, a secret told,
In the fabric of darkness, the brave and bold.
With every heartbeat, the web will sway,
Leading souls along their way.

Tales of wonder softly float,
Like dreams adrift in a fragile boat.
In the midnight web, we dare to tread,
Finding comfort in words unsaid.

Threads of Moonlit Wishes

Under the glow of a silver thread,
Wishes linger where dreams are bred.
With every glimmer, hope takes form,
In moonlit whispers, our hearts grow warm.

We cast our dreams, like seeds in air,
Through tangled branches, we find the rare.
A tapestry stitched with thoughts so bright,
Woven together by the luminous night.

Each wish a star that finds its place,
Glimmering softly, a gentle grace.
In the stillness, magic swirls,
Carried by the breath of the world.

As the night fades, we'll hold them fast,
Threads of moonlit wishes, forever cast.
In every heart, a glimmer remains,
In dreams of night, where hope sustains.

A Pathway Through the Starlit Mirage

Beneath the night, a shimmer glows,
A path unfolds where wonder flows.
Each star a guide, a whispered tune,
In dreams we walk, beneath the moon.

Through misty trails of silver light,
We dance along the edge of night.
The universe, our silent friend,
A journey new that has no end.

With every step, the shadows fade,
And in their place, new worlds are made.
The starlit road through hearts we trace,
A mirage of our own embrace.

So walk with me, where wonders stay,
In endless realms of night and play.
Together, in this sacred space,
We find our path, our rightful place.

The Keeper of Fantasies

In realms where wishes softly weave,
A keeper waits, tasked to believe.
With gentle hands and open heart,
He gathers dreams, a sacred art.

Each whispered hope, a tender song,
In shadows deep where dreams belong.
He guards the light of every star,
Ensuring that our thoughts go far.

When daylight fades and night takes hold,
He lights the fire, fierce and bold.
In whispered winds, our secrets fly,
As fantasies reach for the sky.

So trust the keeper, bold and true,
In every dream, he walks with you.
Together, weave realities,
In lands of love and mysteries.

Silent Wings Above the World

Above the earth, where shadows play,
Silent wings glide, come what may.
They sweep the skies with graceful ease,
A tranquil dance that brings us peace.

In whispered winds, their stories soar,
Through valleys deep and mountains' roar.
With every flap, a tale unfolds,
In quiet realms where courage holds.

Through storm and sun, they carry dreams,
A tapestry of hope that gleams.
With silent strength, they pave the way,
Inviting hearts to join the play.

So lift your gaze and watch them glide,
With open hearts, let love reside.
For in their flight, the world does spin,
And in our souls, the journey begins.

The Silhouette of Forgotten Dreams

Within the shadows, whispers dwell,
Of dreams once bright, they weave a spell.
The silhouettes of hopes long past,
In heart's embrace, their echoes cast.

Beneath the moon, their figures dance,
A fleeting chance, a second glance.
They linger softly, just out of view,
Begging for light to break anew.

With gentle sighs, they touch the air,
Revealing truths we thought were rare.
In silent calls, they seek our grace,
A chance to rise, to find their place.

So heed the night and listen close,
For dreams once lost can still propose.
In every heart, their shadows gleam,
Awakening the forgotten dream.

Weaving Starlit Visions

In the tapestry of night,
Threads of silver gleam and flow,
Dreams are woven, soft and bright,
Guiding where the wishers go.

With each whisper, stars align,
Painting skies with hopes untold,
Every twinkle seems to shine,
Casting visions brave and bold.

Through the silence, shadows dance,
In the glow of moonlit streams,
Every heart is given chance,
To embrace their fleeting dreams.

As the dawn begins to rise,
Fading softly, night departs,
Yet in every waking sigh,
Starlit visions fill our hearts.

The Flight of Fanciful Spirits

In the glade where whispers play,
Fanciful spirits take their flight,
Dancing lightly, night and day,
Chasing echoes out of sight.

With a shimmer in their eyes,
They weave stories through the air,
Gifts of laughter, sweet surprise,
Embroidered dreams beyond compare.

On the breeze, their laughter lingers,
Every flutter speaks of joy,
With their gentle, playful fingers,
Life's a game they will enjoy.

So let your heart embrace the breeze,
Join the spirits in their cheer,
For in wonder, life can seize,
Moments bright that draw us near.

A Lullaby for the Wayward

Close your eyes, the stars will sing,
A lullaby to calm your soul,
Let the night its solace bring,
Filling every aching hole.

In the shadows, dreams take flight,
Softly weaving through the dark,
Like the whispers of the night,
Guiding each and every spark.

Rest your weary thoughts awhile,
Let the tender silence flow,
In this space, you'll find a smile,
Where the gentle breezes blow.

With the dawn, new hope will bloom,
Tears will dry as daylight breaks,
In its glow, dispel the gloom,
And embrace what the heart makes.

Chasing Feathers in the Dark

In the stillness, feathers fall,
Drifting down like whispered sound,
In the night, they softly call,
Luring dreams from all around.

Shadowed paths and whispered sighs,
Through the twilight, echoes roam,
Every secret in disguise,
Leads the spirit safely home.

Chasing visions, wild and free,
In the quiet of the night,
Every flutter speaks to me,
Guiding toward the morning light.

So let the darkness be your guide,
For in shadows, magic stirs,
Chasing feathers, we will glide,
Finding peace as night confers.

The Altar of Starlit Wishes

Beneath the moon's soft silver light,
Whispers gather in the night.
Dreams take flight on hope's warm wings,
In silence, the heart's desire sings.

Stars align like gentle sparks,
Guiding wishes through the dark.
Each twinkle holds a secret prayer,
Echoes of hopes that fill the air.

The altar glimmers with soft gleam,
A sanctuary for every dream.
With every heartbeat, wishes rise,
Carried high in velvet skies.

Beneath the vast, embracing dome,
Every wish finds its way home.
In starlit grace, we seek our bliss,
In night's embrace, we steal a kiss.

Interwoven Tales of Delight

In laughter's dance, our stories weave,
Moments shared, we dare believe.
Each thread a joy, each smile a spark,
Together we light up the dark.

From whispered secrets by the stream,
To painted skies where lovers dream,
Tales of joy, both big and small,
We catch the magic, one and all.

Sunlight filters through the trees,
Carrying tales upon the breeze.
Each moment lived, a treasure bright,
In the fabric of pure delight.

Interwoven hearts embrace the day,
In simple joys, we find our way.
Together we laugh, we sing, we play,
In our woven tales, we shall stay.

The Artistry of Wandering Souls

In quiet paths, our spirits roam,
Seeking places we can call home.
With open hearts, we drift and glide,
In nature's arms, our fears subside.

Mountains call, and rivers flow,
Guided by dreams, we find our flow.
Every detour tells a tale,
In wandering dreams, we set our sail.

Under skies of azure hue,
We chase the moments, bright and true.
With every step, we break the mold,
In the artistry, our souls unfold.

Wandering souls in perfect sync,
Through vibrant landscapes, we shall think.
Each journey shared is a canvas bright,
Painted with love, in purest light.

A Tapestry of Nighttime Whispers

In twilight's hush, the whispers flow,
Secrets shared where soft winds blow.
Threads of stories, dark and light,
Weaving dreams in the silent night.

Comfort found in shadows deep,
Where stars awaken from their sleep.
Each secret held, a treasure rare,
In the stillness, we find our prayer.

The moon a guardian in the sky,
Listening close to our soft sighs.
In this tapestry, we intertwine,
Night's sweet whispers, forever mine.

Together we weave, with gentle grace,
In every heartbeat, a sacred space.
A tapestry of love so near,
In nighttime whispers, all is clear.

The Weaver's Song at Dusk

In twilight's hush, the loom does spin,
Threads of gold, where dreams begin.
Fingers dance in shadows long,
Weaving softly, the weaver's song.

Colors blend, dusk's palette bright,
Fading whispers chase the light.
Each fiber holds a tale untold,
Secrets stitched in hues of gold.

The twilight air, a canvas wide,
Painting stories, where hearts abide.
With every pull, a memory drawn,
The weaver's art from dusk till dawn.

Echoes of Starlit Visions

In the night sky, whispers roam,
Echoes loud, of dreams from home.
Stars align in a cosmic dance,
Lighting paths with every chance.

Visions shine like distant flames,
Casting hopes with whispered names.
In stillness deep, the heart takes flight,
Embracing the magic of the night.

Every twinkle, a tale to tell,
Of love and loss, oh, how they swell.
Under the vast celestial dome,
In starlit whispers, we find our home.

The Keeper of Lost Reveries

In twilight's gleam, she guards the dreams,
A tender heart where silence beams.
With gentle hands, she cradles light,
Keeping lost thoughts from taking flight.

Memories drift like autumn leaves,
In quiet spaces, where one believes.
Patterns of joy, stitched in the air,
In her embrace, they linger there.

Each whispered sigh, a tale to know,
Of kindness shared, and hearts aglow.
The keeper watches, her eyes so wise,
Holding the past beneath the skies.

Night's Embrace

Under the veil of night so deep,
The world bows down, inviting sleep.
In shadows soft, the dreams arise,
Wrapped in starlight, beneath the skies.

A lullaby hums through the air,
Carrying wishes, light as a prayer.
Tucked in clouds, the moonlight glows,
Illuminating paths where wonder flows.

Across the dark, the night unfurls,
Weaving magic, as dreams twirl.
In night's embrace, all fears release,
Here in the stillness, we find our peace.

Wandering Tales

Upon the road where stories weave,
Wandering souls, their hearts believe.
In every step, a whisper's cast,
Echoes linger from the past.

Footsteps soft on ancient ground,
In hidden paths, lost tales are found.
Through forests deep and valleys wide,
Nature cradles, she will abide.

In every turn, a new delight,
Sparks of adventure, igniting the night.
Wandering tales on the winds ride high,
Promising wonders as the years pass by.

Whispers of the Night Sky

Stars twinkle softly, bright and clear,
A gentle breeze whispers secrets near.
The moon drapes silver across the sea,
Embracing shadows, wild and free.

Silence wraps the world in a tender embrace,
Inviting dreams to find their place.
Echoes of the past drift through the air,
In this quiet moment, hearts lay bare.

Under the vastness, worries fade,
In the night's stillness, peace is made.
Each pause a treasure, each sigh a tale,
In the whispers of night, we shall not pale.

With every twinkle, a wish takes flight,
Guided by the stars through the velvet night.
The universe listens, and hope ignites,
In the embrace of the calm, our minds take flight.

Threads of Hope in Moonlight

Woven in twilight, dreams intertwine,
Moonlit pathways, delicate and fine.
A tapestry spun with wishes and grace,
In the heart of silence, they find their place.

Softly they shimmer, the hopes we hold,
In the embrace of night, stories unfold.
Each thread a promise, bright as the dawn,
Guiding us gently, never withdrawn.

Under the watchful gaze of the moon,
Courage awakens, a sweet, tender tune.
In the shadows, our fears retreat,
As threads of joy and love interbeat.

A garden of stars blooms overhead,
With every heartbeat, the night we tread.
In the dance of the cosmos, we find our way,
Threads of hope shining, come what may.

Guardians of the Midnight Realm

In the hush of night, secrets take flight,
Guardians gather, unseen but bright.
With watchful eyes, they guard our dreams,
Cradling wishes in moonlight beams.

Across the skies, whispers arise,
Tales of love and lullabies.
Echoing softly through the trees,
Rustling leaves hum gentle pleas.

Cradled in slumber, we are safe here,
Guarded by spirits, drawing near.
With every breath, a bond is formed,
In the midnight realm, hearts are warmed.

As dawn approaches, shadows retreat,
Yet the guardians' love cannot be beat.
In every heart, their light will stay,
Guiding us softly through the day.

The Tapestry of Slumber

Threads of night weave stories sweet,
In the tapestry of slumber, we meet.
Colors of dreams swirl in the air,
Patterns of peace, beyond compare.

With every breath, the world grows still,
Each moment cradles a wandering will.
In the arms of night, time melts away,
As dreams and silence gently play.

A canvas of starlight, soft and warm,
Embracing the weary, sheltering from harm.
In this sacred space, we find our rest,
With whispers of hope, we are truly blessed.

As dawn breaks softly, dreams will fade,
Yet the tapestry of night is made.
With every slumber, a new tale spun,
In the heart of darkness, we are one.

Silent Guardians of the Night

Beneath the stars, the whispers rise,
Ancient tales in moonlit sighs.
Shadows dance, a gentle sweep,
Silent watch, while the world sleeps.

Hidden paths where secrets lie,
Among the trees, the breezes sigh.
A guardian's call, soft and clear,
Echoes through the night, so near.

Stars align in cosmic flow,
Guiding souls where few may go.
In stillness found, a sense of grace,
In night's embrace, a warm embrace.

With every breath, a fleeting chance,
To lose oneself in night's romance.
Silent guardians, ever strong,
In their midst, we all belong.

Weaving Shadows in the Sky

Threads of dusk in twilight's glow,
Starlit tapestries begin to grow.
A canvas vast, where dreams take flight,
Weaving shadows, painting night.

Clouds like whispers drift and sway,
Carrying secrets from day to day.
In every hue, a story spun,
Through ink-black skies, where hearts run.

The moon, a needle, pierces through,
Stitching stardust, old and new.
Constellations in a dance,
Entwined in night's eternal trance.

Dreamers gaze, their hopes ignite,
In this craft of dark and light.
Weaving shadows with hearts alive,
In the night, we learn to thrive.

Enchanted Pathways of the Mind

Winding routes where thoughts collide,
In the labyrinth of dreams, we hide.
Each twist and turn, a chance to find,
The hidden realms of our own mind.

Through forest paths and river flows,
The whispering winds, the stories grow.
In silence deep, the echoes play,
Enchanted journeys lead the way.

Fragments float in the evening haze,
Guiding us through the complex maze.
With every step, new worlds unfold,
In the mind's embrace, mysteries told.

A tapestry woven, thoughts entwined,
In enchanted pathways of the mind.
Venture forth, with heart and speed,
Each journey starts where dreams may lead.

Fragmented Reflections of Sleep

In the quiet hour, shadows creep,
Starlit fragments dance in sleep.
Fleeting moments, drift away,
Echoes of a dream-filled play.

Whispers soft like velvet night,
Glimmers fade, out of sight.
Thoughts once clear begin to blur,
In fragmented dreams, we stir.

Images swirl like autumn leaves,
In a slumber where the heart believes.
Pieces lost in the dream's embrace,
Reflections shimmering in a quiet space.

As dawn approaches, shadows wane,
Memories of night, touch of rain.
In sleep's embrace, we find our way,
Fragmented reflections, fading gray.

A Symphony of Floating Thoughts

Whispers dance upon the breeze,
Thoughts like leaves in autumn tease.
Melodies drift, soft and light,
Creating harmony in the night.

Breezes hold secrets untold,
In the heart, they unfold.
Dreams take flight, soaring high,
A symphony beneath the sky.

Cascading notes in gentle streams,
Sparkling echoes of our dreams.
Each thought a note in the air,
Playing softly everywhere.

In this symphony, all is found,
A tapestry of joy unbound.
Floating thoughts, a sweet refrain,
Life's music in our veins.

The Lantern in the Dreaming Woods

In the woods where shadows creep,
A lantern glows, secrets to keep.
It flickers bright in the night air,
Guiding souls with gentle care.

Through tangled trees and winding trails,
The light persists, it never fails.
Whispers of magic, ancient and wise,
Illuminate wonders before our eyes.

Each step reveals a hidden path,
Where dreams emerge from shadow's wraths.
The lantern's glow, a beacon true,
Awakens hope in hearts anew.

In the dreaming woods, we roam,
With every flicker, we feel at home.
The light will lead us, come what may,
Through the depths where dreams hold sway.

Echoes in the Fabric of Night

In the dark where silence reigns,
Echoes whisper through the chains.
Stars blink down, a distant lore,
Painting shadows on the floor.

Threads of time weave tales unknown,
In the fabric, we have grown.
Each memory a stitch in place,
In the night's cool embrace.

Voices murmur in the vast,
Carrying whispers of the past.
In the stillness, echoes call,
Beneath the sky, we feel them all.

The fabric of night holds our fears,
And the laughter shared through years.
In these echoes, we find light,
Illuminating the quiet night.

Moonlit Trail of Silent Wishes

Along the path where moonbeams play,
Silent wishes drift away.
Each step upon the silvered trail,
Carries dreams like a whispered tale.

Stars above twinkle and shine,
Guiding hearts drawn like a line.
With each wish upon the breeze,
Hope awakens and finds its ease.

The quiet night wraps us tight,
With a cloak of soft, gentle light.
On this trail, our spirits soar,
As wishes linger, forevermore.

In the moonlit glow, we find our truth,
Nurtured softly, the dreams of youth.
With every wish cast in the night,
The world becomes a canvas bright.

Streams of Consciousness Flowing

Thoughts like water gently stream,
They dance and swirl, a timeless theme.
In quiet corners, secrets seep,
Unraveled whispers, dreams we keep.

Fleeting moments drift away,
In currents where our hopes do sway.
A tapestry of light and shade,
In the flow, the mind is laid.

Echoes call from depths unseen,
In every ripple, truths convene.
Ideas drift on warming tides,
Through endless flow, the spirit glides.

Join the stream, let worries cease,
In this movement, find your peace.
With each thought, a new world grows,
In the flow, the heart just knows.

The Scribe of Varied Dreamscapes

With ink of night and dawn's delight,
The scribe pens tales in soft moonlight.
Each dreamscape swirls with vibrant hues,
In realms where reality bends and views.

Mountains rise beneath velvet skies,
Whispers of hope in each sunrise.
Through forests deep and oceans wide,
Imagination's wings, our only guide.

In shadows cast by fleeting stars,
The scribe unveils both scars and scars.
With every stroke, a world is born,
In fantastical realms, we are reborn.

As tales unfold on parchment bare,
Let your heart roam without care.
For in these dreams, we find our way,
Through the scribe's pen, we dance and play.

Hushed Murmurs of the Universe

In stillness lies the cosmic song,
A melody that swells so strong.
The stars hum soft, a gentle tune,
Awakening thoughts beneath the moon.

Galaxies whisper ancient lore,
Secrets held in tales of yore.
Of time and space, a breathless pause,
In every atom, life's great cause.

With every heartbeat, echoes swell,
A universe within, we dwell.
In hallowed silence, truths arise,
In hushed murmurs, wisdom lies.

Let the cosmos pull you near,
In the vastness, shed your fear.
Embrace the stillness, feel the grace,
In whispers soft, find your place.

Fables of the Wandering Heart

Across the world, the heart does roam,
In search of love, it feels like home.
With echoes of laughter in the air,
Each step unfolds a tale to share.

Mountains climbed and rivers crossed,
Each journey rich, though sometimes lost.
In every face, a story glows,
The wandering heart's path ever grows.

Through valleys deep and skies of blue,
In fleeting moments, friendships brew.
With every fable, hearts ignite,
Guided by dreams that take to flight.

So wander far, let your spirit soar,
Embrace the world, and seek for more.
In the tales we weave, the heart shall find,
A love that binds all humankind.

Twilight's Secret Passage

In the hush of fading light,
Whispers dance in soft twilight.
Colors blend, a gentle sigh,
Magic weaves as day bids bye.

Footsteps trace the silent path,
Where shadows greet the aftermath.
Lurking mysteries, half-revealed,
In night's embrace, hearts are healed.

Stars awaken, peeking through,
Guiding dreams in shades of blue.
Through the veil, the secrets flow,
Twilight's gift, a soothing glow.

Time stands still at this sweet hour,
Where the ordinary turns to power.
In every breath, a world anew,
Twilight sings, and whispers true.

The Harmony of Untold Stories

In the silence of the night,
Every star's a distant light.
Echoes of a life once lived,
Tales of joy and pain, heaved.

Pages turning in the breeze,
Ancient truths on whispered knees.
Voices blend, a soft refrain,
Carving paths through heart and brain.

Hidden dreams, like rivers flow,
In the quiet, secrets grow.
Harmonies of joy and strife,
Nestled deep within our life.

With each story that we find,
Threads of fate become entwined.
In the tapestry of fate,
Untold tales illuminate.

Mosaics of Midnight Shadows

Underneath the silver glow,
Shadows weave a dance of woe.
Fragments scatter on the ground,
Mosaic patterns spin around.

Each silhouette tells a tale,
Of whispered hopes that wane and pale.
Stories etched in dark's embrace,
In each corner, a hidden trace.

Night's soft quilt, a cover vast,
Memories fade, but never past.
In the shadows, dreams unfold,
A canvas painted with the bold.

Mysteries held in midnight's sway,
Colors blend, then gently fray.
In the stillness, silence sings,
Of the beauty that darkness brings.

The Bridge to Otherworlds

Across the stream where waters twine,
A bridge appears, old yet divine.
Steps adorned with ancient lore,
Calling hearts to venture more.

Glimmers of a world unseen,
Where dreams lie veiled in tranquil green.
Curious whispers urge to tread,
To cross the threshold, leave the thread.

Each step taken banishes fear,
An echo of futures drawing near.
Mystical realms invite the bold,
Tales unravel, secrets unfold.

In every crack, a story waits,
Journey onward, open gates.
With every breath, horizons blend,
A bridge between each heart and end.

Flight of the Gossamer Spirits

In twilight's hush, they gently rise,
With whispered wings, they touch the skies.
Woven with light, they dance in air,
Elusive shadows, free of care.

Through fields of stardust, softly glint,
Their laughter echoes, a silken hint.
Lost in the breeze, they twirl and sway,
Enchanting all who watch their play.

Each flicker bright, a fleeting dream,
A glimpse of hope, a silver stream.
They guide the weary, calm their fears,
In their embrace, the soul endears.

To love and wonder, they pave our way,
In gentle spirals, they weave and sway.
Flight of gossamer, a soft caress,
In realms of magic, we find our blessed.

Beneath the Veil of Dreamscapes

Where shadows dance on whispered sighs,
Beneath the veil, the magic lies.
In twilight's glow, the secrets bloom,
As dreamers wander through the gloom.

A tapestry of starlit night,
Weaving tales in softest light.
Each step a heartbeat, a pulse unknown,
In scattered echoes, truths are sown.

With every heartbeat, a vision glows,
Where the silent river of dreaming flows.
Past veils of wonder, we chase the gleam,
In the cradle of night, we soar and dream.

Beneath the veil, we rise and fall,
Each whispered wish, a distant call.
In the depths of dreams, our spirits play,
Guided by starlight, we find our way.

Tales Stitched in Silver Light

In the weavings of time, stories reside,
Tales stitched of silver, where shadows glide.
Each moment captured, a memory spun,
In threads of wonder, we are one.

Whispers of ages, calling us near,
Echoing softly, the songs we hear.
In the twilight tapestry, colors blend,
A dance of stories, where beginnings end.

The moonlight bathes the narratives bright,
Each stitch a dream, a fleeting sight.
Bound by the threads of our shared night,
In silvered echoes, we take our flight.

From love to loss, each tale profound,
In the heart's fabric, we are unbound.
Tales stitched in silver, we carry inside,
As glow of memories, we cannot hide.

A Journey Through the Ethereal Veil

Through realms unseen, our spirits roam,
A journey embarked, far from home.
With stars as guides, we venture forth,
To realms of wonder, a sacred birth.

In ethereal mist, shadows unfold,
Whispers of secrets waiting, untold.
Each step a heartbeat, a timeless dance,
In the embrace of dreams, we chance.

Across the horizon, where dawn meets dusk,
In the twilight's shimmer, we find our trust.
A journey woven with starlight's grace,
Through the veil of night, we find our place.

With every breath, the cosmos sings,
In ethereal realms, our spirit springs.
Forever wandering, we chase the flame,
A journey sacred, never the same.

Realm of Surreal Wanderings

In a land where dreams unfold,
Colors swirl and tales are told.
Whispers dance upon the air,
Magic lingers everywhere.

Shadows stretch and gently sway,
Guiding lost souls on their way.
Footsteps soft on mystic ground,
Echoes of the lost are found.

Stars ignite the velvet sky,
Where wishes float and spirits fly.
Bridges built of hope and light,
Lead us through the starry night.

Every turn, a secret waits,
Opening ancient, hidden gates.
Realm of dreams, a wondrous place,
Where hearts can find their gentle grace.

The Kiss of Sleepy Shadows

In twilight's gentle, soft embrace,
The world slows down, finds its place.
Shadows creep and softly sigh,
Underneath the velvet sky.

Whispers weave through tangled trees,
Carried softly on the breeze.
Moonlight casts a silver veil,
While love's secrets gently sail.

Dreams entwined in tender grace,
Find their home in this still space.
With each breath, the night unfolds,
A tender kiss that time withholds.

Resting softly, hushed and deep,
In this lullaby's sweet keep.
Let the shadows hold you tight,
In the arms of peaceful night.

Tapestry of Starlit Reverie

Weaving threads of shimmering light,
A tapestry of dreams at night.
Each star a stitch, a tale to share,
Stories woven in the air.

Nature's canvas, vast and grand,
Painted by a gentle hand.
Colors whisper, bright and bold,
Echoing secrets from the old.

Floating ships on clouds of thought,
In this realm, all fear is naught.
Reflections dance on silver streams,
Where we're lost in woven dreams.

In this night, our hearts align,
Within the stars, our souls entwine.
A dreamer's paradise awaits,
As we unravel all life's fates.

Chasing Phantoms in the Night

Silent whispers fill the air,
Echoes of what once was there.
Chasing shadows, fleeting, light,
In the depth of endless night.

Memories swirl like autumn leaves,
In the breeze, a heart believes.
Phantom figures softly glide,
Through the places we once cried.

Each step taken, time unwinds,
Revealing truths that fate defines.
In the dark, the past calls out,
With stories lost and wrapped in doubt.

But in this chase, we find our way,
Through the echoes of the day.
Phantoms fade with morning light,
Leaving dreams in silent flight.

Caught Between Realms

In twilight's grasp, I stand in pause,
An echo whispers, without a cause.
The stars above, a flickering dance,
While shadows blend, a fickle romance.

Dreams entwined in a silken thread,
Paths unknown where the cautious tread.
Between the worlds, I drift and sway,
Caught in the night, till break of day.

Voices call from the edges near,
A haunting tune that draws me near.
In the space where light meets dark,
I seek a truth, a whispering spark.

As dawn approaches, colors blend,
Bridging the gap where forces send.
Caught in the surreal, I find my place,
A fleeting moment, an endless space.

Echoes of Lost Wishes

In silent woods, where shadows play,
Lost wish echoes drift away.
Once vibrant dreams in the boughs of time,
Now mere whispers, a half-forgotten rhyme.

Moonlit nights unveil the sighs,
Of distant hopes beneath vast skies.
Stars above, they gleam and fade,
Marking the paths where dreams once laid.

With every breeze, a chance reborn,
Yet lost in layers, we mourn the worn.
Memories twinkle like fireflies bright,
Fleeting sparks in the depth of night.

To chase those echoes, we wander far,
Through winding paths, beneath each star.
In the heart of the forest, wishes reside,
Seeking solace, where dreams abide.

Silken Veils of the Subconscious

Behind silken veils, the shadows lie,
Where thoughts meander, and dreams can fly.
A labyrinth formed from delicate threads,
Weaving the night where the mind dreads.

Lost in a whisper, time stands still,
Chasing reflections, a nameless thrill.
Each layer reveals a hidden glance,
In the depths of a comforting trance.

Fleeting visions like dancers weave,
In twilight's grasp, they softly breathe.
Within this realm of the unspoken,
A world of wonders and dreams unbroken.

In the quiet corners, mysteries dwell,
Veils of the mind, a potent spell.
To venture deeper, where few will tread,
Silken dreams cradle, all fears shed.

The Path of Ethereal Shadows

Upon a path of ethereal grace,
Shadows linger in a timeless space.
Whispers of night beckon me close,
Guiding my steps where the dreamers doze.

Moonlight bathes the trail in silver,
As secrets of dusk and dawn converge.
Footfalls echo through the quiet glade,
Where shadows dance, in twilight's parade.

Fleeting moments weave the soft air,
A tapestry rich with tales to share.
The stars, like lanterns, guide my way,
Illuminating paths where dreams sway.

In this realm where the heartbeats blend,
Finding solace in shadows that mend.
Ethereal trails where the lost can find,
A connection deep, of spirit and mind.

The Lantern's Path to Dreaming

Upon the lane where shadows play,
A lantern's glow lights up the way.
Each flicker tells a tale untold,
Of dreams that wander brave and bold.

As whispers dance on evening's breath,
They weave a spell of life and death.
Through misty veils the visions roam,
In twilight's arms, they find their home.

A guiding light in realms unknown,
Where fears dissolve and love has grown.
With every step, the heart takes flight,
On paths adorned in silver light.

In slumber's tender embrace, we find,
The world transformed, peace intertwined.
So walk this path, let dreams unfurl,
With lanterns bright, explore the world.

Silken Pathways Under Starry Skies

Beneath the stars, the night unspools,
Where silken threads weave tales like jewels.
Each shimmer holds a wish, a dream,
A cosmic dance, a silver gleam.

Through velvet night, the pathways sigh,
As moonlight spills, the shadows fly.
In this embrace, the heart beats true,
With every step, the soul renews.

Among the whispers of the breeze,
The secrets hide behind the trees.
While dreams take form in gentle light,
We wander forth, hearts pure and bright.

In harmony with stars above,
We tread the path, we seek the love.
Each moment lives within our eyes,
As silken pathways lead to skies.

Where Night's Secrets Dwell

In moonlit groves where shadows thrive,
The night unfolds, the secrets dive.
With every rustle, something stirs,
The quiet world, a dream concurs.

Beneath the boughs, the silence sighs,
The whispers drift like soft goodbyes.
In hidden corners, wonders creep,
Where magic lingers, dreams are deep.

Here, starlit echoes softly call,
A tapestry of night enthralls.
The stories woven in the air,
Reveal the truths we long to share.

Where shadows cast their gentle shroud,
The heart can beat both loud and proud.
In every dark, a spark will glow,
For in the night, our spirits flow.

Timeless Whispers of the Nocturne

As evening falls, the world grows still,
Timeless whispers echo at will.
In soft refrain, the stars reply,
While dreams take flight, the heart can fly.

Through dusky shades, the melodies weave,
In every sigh, the night deceives.
With silver tones, the darkness sings,
Of mystery and hidden things.

Each note is wrapped in twilight's grace,
A fleeting glimpse of time and space.
In this embrace, forever seems,
A dance of shadows, hopes, and dreams.

So raise your voice, let echoes ring,
In moonlit halls where spirits cling.
In timeless breaths, we find our way,
Through nocturne's charm, we'll always stay.

The Art of Letting Go

In quiet moments, I release,
The weight of dreams, a gentle peace.
Each memory fades, like autumn's leaf,
Embracing change, in sweet relief.

I watch the tides, they ebb and flow,
Like whispers soft, they come, they go.
With every breath, I learn to trust,
The art of letting go is just.

No chains to bind, no fears to hold,
In warmth of sun, my heart unfolds.
I shed the past, a fragile thread,
To dance anew, the path ahead.

In twilight's grace, I find my strength,
A journey long, yet full in breadth.
With open hands and heart set free,
I mold my fate, just wait and see.

Cradled by Moonlit Dreams

Underneath a silver glow,
Where shadows weave and breezes blow.
I drift away on whispered beams,
Cradled soft by moonlit dreams.

Stars twinkling in the inky night,
Guiding hearts with gentle light.
Each sigh that fades, a soft caress,
In silence found, I find my rest.

The world awakes in softest hues,
In slumber deep, I chase my muse.
With every glance, the heavens gleam,
As I am lost in moonlit dreams.

I wander through the starlit skies,
With hope aglow in my bright eyes.
In the night's embrace, I find my way,
Cradled in dreams until the day.

Beneath the Whispering Pines

In forests deep, where secrets lie,
Beneath the pines that touch the sky.
The breeze it carries tales untold,
In nature's heart, my soul I hold.

Each rustling leaf, a soothing song,
A melody where I belong.
With every step on mossy ground,
I find the peace that can be found.

The sunbeams dance through branches high,
Illuminating earth and sky.
In shadowed quiet, I will stay,
Beneath the pines, I lose my way.

In whispered vows, the wild things speak,
To share the strength of those who seek.
Among the trees, my heart aligns,
With every breath, beneath the pines.

A Passage to the Other Side

On misty paths where shadows fade,
A passage waits, for dreams are made.
With every step, the world unwinds,
A whisper calls from other kinds.

The veil so thin, the light will break,
A journey starts, for love's own sake.
With open heart, I'll take the leap,
Into the deep, where secrets keep.

The stars align, the night ignites,
A canvas vast of endless sights.
With every breath, a promise glides,
Across the stream to the other sides.

In timeless grace, I'll find my way,
Through realms of light, where spirits play.
Beyond the veil, the truth abides,
A passage wide to the other sides.

Dance of the Wandering Memories

In shadows cast by twilight's grace,
Whispers echo in a familiar place.
The laughter of days, like leaves in flight,
Weaves through the tapestry of night.

Footsteps traced on forgotten paths,
Breathe life into long-lost laughs.
Each moment swirls, a fragrant breeze,
In memory's dance, the heart finds ease.

Beneath the stars that softly gleam,
Fragments of time weave a silent dream.
Past and present in a soft embrace,
A waltz of wonder, a timeless grace.

In the twilight's gentle sigh,
We let the echoes softly fly.
Dance on, dear heart, let shadows play,
In the wandering memories, we'll forever stay.

Embrace of the Dream Weaver

Through the veil where dreams unfold,
A weaver crafts stories untold.
Threads of starlight, colors bright,
Embraced within the silent night.

In whispered hopes and gentle sighs,
The heart's desires softly rise.
A canvas painted with wishes sheer,
In this moment, all is clear.

Embrace the dance of what may come,
In the rhythm of a gentle drum.
Every dream, a spark divine,
In the weaver's art, our souls align.

So close your eyes, let visions flow,
In the embrace where dreamers go.
A world awaits, both vast and near,
In the weaver's arms, we've naught to fear.

Beneath the Celestial Canopy

Underneath the stars' soft glow,
A world of wonders starts to show.
Galaxies spin, a cosmic dance,
Inviting hearts to dream and chance.

Constellations whisper tales of old,
Of warriors brave and treasures bold.
The moonlight sparkles on the sea,
A lullaby for you and me.

In the night, our spirits rise,
Beneath the vast and endless skies.
With every twinkle, wishes fly,
In the universe, you and I.

So take my hand, let's drift away,
To where the night can softly sway.
Beneath this canopy, we'll find,
The secrets held by stars entwined.

The Soul's Nighttime Voyage

In the quiet hush of midnight's veil,
The soul embarks on a whispered trail.
Through realms unseen, it softly glides,
As cosmic currents become its guides.

With every star, a story born,
Of love and loss, of dreams forlorn.
Exploring depths of worlds anew,
Where shadows blend with morning's hue.

In stardust realms, fears dissipate,
In the stillness, we navigate.
Each heartbeat echoes, a gentle sound,
In the voyage, lost souls are found.

So close your eyes and drift away,
Let the night hold you, come what may.
In the soul's embrace, we are alive,
On this nighttime voyage, we will thrive.

Cords of Destiny in Twilight

In twilight's grace, the shadows weave,
Threads of fate we can't perceive.
Whispers call from realms unknown,
Binding souls in twilight's tone.

Stars hang low, a tapestry bright,
Guiding dreams through the night.
Cords of destiny gently sway,
Carving paths where heartbeats play.

Each moment holds a fleeting chance,
In the dance of fate's strange glance.
As time drips like melting gold,
Stories of the brave unfold.

With hope as our unwavering guide,
We walk the edge where dreams collide.
In twilight's arms, we find our way,
Embracing night that turns to day.

The Silhouette of a Fading Dream

In the hush of night, a shadow stands,
Draped in whispers, like shifting sands.
A fading dream, it flickers bright,
In the corners of my mind's soft light.

Echoes linger of laughter lost,
Bound by memories, the heart's cost.
Each breath a sigh, a soft farewell,
To the stories time dared not tell.

Moonlight weaves through branches bare,
Seeking solace in the air.
The silhouette fades with the dawn,
A fleeting vision, now withdrawn.

Yet in the silence, hope remains,
To awaken dreams from gentle chains.
With every dawn, a spark ignites,
Reviving visions in morning lights.

Voyage Beyond the Veil

Set sail on seas of silver mist,
Where whispers of the past persist.
Beyond the veil, we seek and roam,
In the embrace of the unknown.

Charting paths with stars aligned,
To the rhythms of heart and mind.
Each wave a tale, each gust a song,
Guiding spirits where they belong.

In depths uncharted, secrets lie,
Beneath the vast and endless sky.
With courage as our steadfast guide,
We embark where dreams reside.

Through storms and calm, we find our way,
In unity, we seize the day.
Voyage beyond, let spirits soar,
Together we discover more.

The Light That Dances in Shadows

In twilight's hush, a flicker glows,
A secret light that softly flows.
It dances playfully in the night,
Bringing warmth, dispelling fright.

Among the shadows, it leaps and twirls,
Spinning stories, unfurling pearls.
A gentle glow that finds its way,
Through darkened corners, brightening day.

Faint echoes of laughter trail behind,
Illuminating paths for the blind.
In every heart, it leaves a trace,
A testament to hope and grace.

So let it shine through trials fierce,
In every moment, let it pierce.
The light that dances, ever bold,
A beacon for the brave and the old.

Milton Keynes UK
Ingram Content Group UK Ltd.
UKHW021207261024
450281UK00007B/77

9 789916 906040